What Living Things Need

Air

Vic Parker

www.raintreepublishers.co.uk
Visit our website to find out more information about **Raintree** books.

To order:
☎ Phone 44 (0) 1865 888112
Send a fax to 44 (0) 1865 314091
Visit the Raintree Bookshop at **www.raintreepublishers.co.uk** to browse our catalogue and order online.

First published in Great Britain by Raintree, Halley Court, Jordan Hill, Oxford OX2 8EJ, part of Harcourt Education.
Raintree is a registered trademark of Harcourt Education Ltd.

First published in paperback in 2007.

Editorial: Jilly Attwood and Kathy Peltan
Design: Jo Hinton-Malivoire and Bigtop
Picture Research: Ruth Blair and Andrea Sadler
Production: Séverine Ribierre

Originated by Modern Age House Ltd, Hong Kong
Printed and bound in China by South China Printing Company

10 digit ISBN 1 406 20034 4 (hardback)
13 digit ISBN 978 1 406 20034 8

11 10 09 08 07 06
10 9 8 7 6 5 4 3 2 1

10 digit ISBN 1 406 20040 9 (paperback)
13 digit ISBN 978 1 406 20040 9

11 10 09 08
10 9 8 7 6 5 4 3

British Library Cataloguing in Publication Data
Parker, Victoria
Air. – (What living things need)
572.4′7
A full catalogue record for this book is available from the British Library.

Acknowledgements
The publishers would like to thank the following for permission to reproduce photographs: Corbis pp. **6**, **7**, **8**, **14** (John Conrad), back cover (kite); FLPA p. **4** (David Hosking); FLPA (Minden Pictures) pp. **15**, **16**, **23** (insects); Getty Images p. 5; Getty Images (Digital Vision) pp. **12**, **19**, **23** (gills); Getty Images (Photodisc) pp. **11**, **17**, **23** (breathe), back cover (butterfly); Getty Images (Stone) pp. **13**, **23** (oxygen); Getty Images (Taxi) pp. **22**, **23** (air tank); NHPA (Martin Harvey) p. **21**; Photofusion p. **10** (Paul Baldesere), **20** (J. Chapman); TopFoto pp. **9** (Ellen B Senisi, The Image Works), **18** (Avampini, V&W, The Image Works).

Cover photograph reproduced with permission of Alamy.

The publishers would like to thank Michael Scott for his assistance in the preparation of this book.

Contents

Some words are shown in bold, **like this**. You can find them in the picture glossary on page 23.

What is a living thing?

Living things are things that grow.

People, animals, and plants are living things.

Which things in this picture are living and which are not?

What is air?

Air is all around us.

But you cannot see, smell, or taste air.

You can feel air moving when you are on a swing.

Do we need air?

We need air to talk, think,
and move.

We need air to grow.

How does air get inside us?

You take air into your body through your nose and mouth.

This is called breathing.

You **breathe** air out again that way too.

Do we need air all the time?

We need air all the time.

We **breathe** air without thinking about it.

Air has **oxygen** in it. You cannot live without oxygen for long.

Hold your breath and see.

Do animals need air?

All living things need air.

Many animals **breathe** through their nose and mouth, like we do.

Do you know the name for
a bird's mouth?

Do all animals breathe like us?

Not all animals **breathe** like us.

Insects have mouths but they use them just for eating.

Insects do not have noses.

They breathe through tiny holes in their bodies.

Can animals breathe underwater?

Some animals need to hold their breath when they go underwater.

This whale is coming up for air.

Fish can **breathe** underwater. They get **oxygen** from the water.

Fish breathe through openings called **gills**.

How do plants breathe?

Plants do not **breathe** like people.

They take in air through tiny holes in their leaves.

All plants take in air.

Little flowers take in air.
So do big, tall trees.

Can you guess?

Can you guess how this person is breathing underwater?

He is using an **air tank**.

Glossary

air tank a metal box filled with air with a tube to your mouth, so you can breathe underwater

breathe pull air into and out of the body

gills openings in a fish's body where air from the water goes in and out

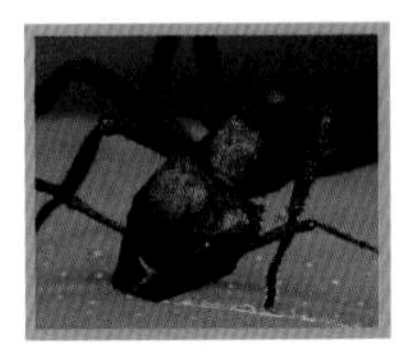

insects animals with six legs, such as beetles

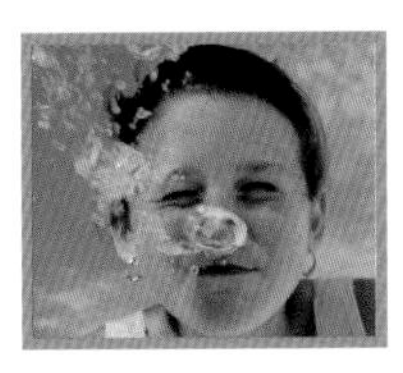

oxygen part of air

Index

Note to parents and teachers

Reading non-fiction texts for information is an important part of a child's literacy development. Readers can be encouraged to ask simple questions and then use the text to find the answers. Most chapters in this book begin with a question. Read the questions together. Look at the pictures. Talk about what the answer might be. Then read the text to find out if your predictions were correct. To develop readers' enquiry skills, encourage them to think of other questions they might ask about the topic. Discuss where you could find the answers. Assist children in using the contents page, picture glossary and index to practise research skills and new vocabulary.